EARTH CYCLES

SEASONS

Sally Morgan

FRANKLIN WATTS

This edition 2012

First published in 2009 by Franklin Watts
338 Euston Road
London NW1 3BH

Franklin Watts Australia
Level 17/207 Kent Street
Sydney, NSW 2000

Copyright © Franklin Watts 2009
All rights reserved

Editor: Jean Coppendale
Design: Paul Manning

Produced for Franklin Watts by
White-Thomson Publishing Ltd

www.wtpub.co.uk
+44 (0) 845 362 8240

A CIP catalogue record for this book is available from the British Library.

ISBN 978 1 4451 0788 2

Dewey classification: 508.2

Picture credits

t = top b = bottom l = left = r = right
3r, 14b, ECO/Angela Hampton; 3l, 14r, Shutterstock/Asharkyu; 4 main, Shutterstock/Lakov Kalinin; 4l, 4r, ECO/Stuart Baines; 5l, 5b, Stuart Baines; 5r, Shutterstock/Andrzej Gibasiewicz; 6l, ECO/Anthony Cooper; 6r, Shutterstock/Arnon Ayal; 7l, Shutterstock/K. Kaplin; 7r, ECO/Josef Stuefer; 8 (diagram), Stefan Chabluk; 9, Shutterstock/Joe Ng; 10t (diagram), Stefan Chabluk; 10b, Shutterstock/Raisa Kanareva; 11l, ECO/Fritz Polking; llr, Shutterstock/Stephen Aaron Rees; 12, Shutterstock/David Davis; 12 (diagram), Stefan Chabluk; 12b, Shutterstock/Gordana Sermek; 13l, Michael Nguyen; 13r, Shutterstock/Gordana Sermek; 15l, ECO/David Wootton Photography; 16b, 30b, Shutterstock/Marek Mierzejewski; 16r, Shutterstock/Shchipkova Elena; 17t, ECO/Robert Picket; 17b, Shutterstock/Pichugin Dmitry; 18, Shutterstock/Yuriy Kulyk; 18b, Shutterstock/Fotosav; 19t, Shutterstock/Brenda Carson; 19b,31, Shutterstock/Pawel Strykowski; 19r, Shutterstock/Goran Cakmazovic; 20l, Shutterstock/Gallimaufry; 20r, Shutterstock/Romanchuck Dimitry; 21l, Shutterstock/Grafikfoto; 21b, Shutterstock/ Kristian Sekulic; 21t, ECO/Peter Cairns; 22b, Shutterstock/EcoPrint; 22t, Shutterstock/Pichugin Dmitry; 23b, Shutterstock/Gail Johnson; 23r, Shutterstock/Four Oaks; 24, Shutterstock/Marc van Vuren; 24t, Shutterstock/Juriah Mosin; 25l, Shutterstock/Vera Bogaerts; 25r, ECO/Chinch Gryniewicz; 26l, ECO/Chinch Gryniewicz; 26r, ECO/Phillip Colla; 27l, ECO/Robin Redfern; 27r, ECO/Bryan Knox; 28b, Shutterstock/Piotr Majka; 28t, ECO/Steven Gazlowski; 29b, Peter Cairns; 29t, Laura Sivell; 29r, Reinhard Dirscherl; 30t, Shutterstock/Borislav Borisov.
Cover image: Shutterstock/Mikael Damkier

Note to parents and teachers
Every effort has been made by the Publishers to ensure that the websites listed on page 32 are suitable for children, that they are of the highest educational value and that they contain no inappropriate or offensive material. However, because of the nature of the Internet, it is impossible to guarantee that the contents of these sites will not been altered. We strongly advise that Internet access is supervised by a responsible adult.

Printed in China

Franklin Watts is a division of Hachette Children's Books,
an Hachette UK company
www.hachette.co.uk

Contents

Words appearing in **bold** like this can be found
in the Glossary on pages 30-31.

Climate and weather

A year is usually divided into parts called **seasons**. A season is a regular change in the weather that happens each year at about the same time. Each season has a particular pattern of weather, for example winters in northern Europe are usually cold and wet.

Weather

Weather and **climate** are not the same. Weather is the day-to-day temperature, rainfall and wind. It is always changing. One minute the weather can be dry and sunny, the next it can be windy and cloudy with rain.

▼ Europe's climate has four seasons. The photographs below show the four seasons in a European woodland.

1
Spring

2
Summer

Climate

The word 'climate' refers to the regular pattern of weather over the year. The climate of a place depends on many things, such as its distance from the **Equator**, whether there are mountains or whether it lies close to the ocean. For example, the climate experienced right in the middle of North America is very different from that along the Pacific or Atlantic coasts.

Q Have climates always been the same?

A No. Climates have changed over time. For example, Northern Europe was much warmer 1,000 years ago. When the **Vikings** discovered Greenland they found green fields and forests. Now the climate is much colder, with a lot of the land covered in snow all year round.

3
Autumn

4
Winter

▲ Greenland was once covered with green fields and forests.

Seasonal climates

Seasons vary around the world. In the **tropics** there are small differences between the seasons, but at the **poles**, the seasons are very different.

Tropical climates

The tropics lie either side of the Equator. Here, seasonal changes are less noticeable because it is hot all year round. Some tropical places have a hot and wet climate all year round, with small differences in rainfall. Other parts of the tropics have two seasons: a dry season and a wet season.

▶ These orchids need warm, wet conditions, so they grow well in tropical climates.

▶ Many people like to take holidays in tropical places where it is hot and sunny most days.

Q and A

Temperate zones

The **temperate zone** lies between the tropics and the poles. There are usually four seasons here — spring, summer, autumn and winter. The seasons differ in day length, temperature and patterns of rainfall.

Polar climates

The poles experience two extremely different seasons. One is summer, when the Sun is above the horizon. The days are long and temperatures rise just above freezing. The other is winter, when the Sun dips below the horizon. It is dark for much of the time and temperatures fall well below freezing.

Q What is the Midnight Sun?

A The Midnight Sun is seen at the poles in summer. It occurs during the middle of summer when the Sun never sets below the horizon, so it is still light during the middle of the night.

▲ Midnight Sun over the coast of Finland.

▼ The Antarctic has a polar climate. It is covered in snow and ice even in summer.

Spinning around the Sun

The seasons are caused by the way the Earth **orbits** or spins around the Sun.

The seasons

The Earth takes a year to orbit the Sun. The Earth does not lie at right angles to the Sun, but is tilted at an angle of 23.5°. This means that for half of the year, the North Pole is tilted towards the Sun, and for the second half of the year, the South Pole is tilted towards the Sun. It is this tilt that creates the seasons.

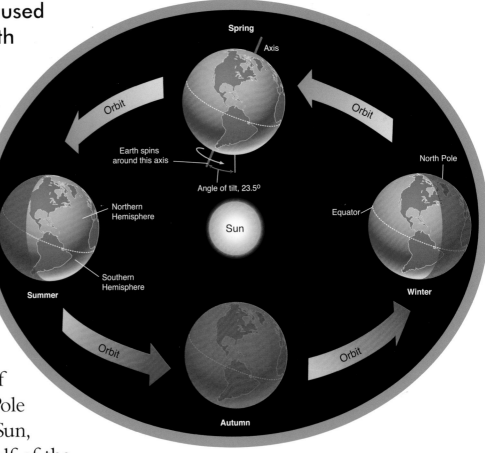

▲ The Earth spins around its axis. The axis is an imaginary line that runs through the centre of the Earth from the North to the South Pole. The diagram above shows how the axis is tilted, so that different parts of the Earth are angled towards the Sun at different times of the year.

Summer or winter?

The **Northern Hemisphere** has summer when the Earth is tilted towards the Sun and winter when it is tilted away. The **Southern Hemisphere** has the opposite pattern, so when it is summer in the north, it is winter in the south.

Day and night

As the Earth orbits the Sun, it spins **anticlockwise**, from east to west. A complete spin takes 24 hours, which is the length of a day. As the Earth spins, one side is facing the Sun and is receiving sunlight, while the other side is pointing away from the Sun and is in darkness. This creates the daily cycle of day and night.

Q Is the Earth's spin slowing down?

A Yes. The Earth is very gradually spinning more slowly. Scientists have found that about 400 million years ago a day was only 22 hours long. Since then, the Earth has slowed down by a fraction of a second every 100 years.

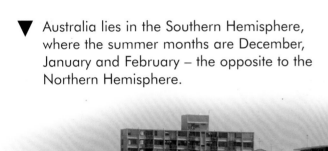

▼ Australia lies in the Southern Hemisphere, where the summer months are December, January and February – the opposite to the Northern Hemisphere.

Hot and cold

The position of the Sun overhead varies during the year, and this influences the weather.

Sun's rays

Sun

Equator

Earth

Earth's axis

Polar region

Temperate zone

Tropical zone

Temperate zone

Polar region

Tropical heat

In the tropics, the Sun is always high in the sky and rays of sunlight hit the Earth's surface directly, heating the ground. Some parts of the tropics get plenty of rain, but others get very little, for example deserts. Heat from the Sun also warms the surface of the oceans, and this sets up **currents**, where water flows from one place to another.

▲ At the Equator the Sun's rays have less distance to travel to reach the Earth so there is more heat. At the poles, the rays travel further and so have less heat.

► Camels can survive the heat of deserts and go for many weeks without drinking.

Q and A

Polar cold

In the polar regions, the Sun is low in the sky even in summer. The Sun's rays have to pass through a lot of **atmosphere** (the layer of gases around the Earth) before they hit the ground at an angle. The rays are spread out over a large area and there is little heat left. The white snow and ice **reflect** the heat, too. For these reasons it is always cold in the polar regions, even in summer.

Q What is the Gulf Stream?

A The Gulf Stream is a current of warm water that flows across the Atlantic from Florida to Norway. It helps to create a mild climate for much of north-west Europe including the UK. Without it, the climate would be much colder.

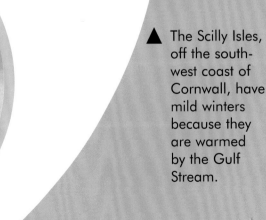

▼ Emperor penguins live near the South Pole, where the winters are long, dark and cold.

▲ The Scilly Isles, off the south-west coast of Cornwall, have mild winters because they are warmed by the Gulf Stream.

Day length

In the tropics, the Sun is overhead all year round and there are 12 hours of daylight and 12 hours of night. However, day length varies considerably elsewhere.

Changes in day length

In the temperate zone, day length changes through each season. This is caused by the way the Earth is tilted towards the Sun. In spring, the Sun starts to get higher in the sky, so the days become longer. The longest days occur in summer and become shorter as autumn approaches. Each day, the midday Sun is a little lower in the sky. In winter, the Sun rises later and sets earlier. There are only about eight hours of daylight.

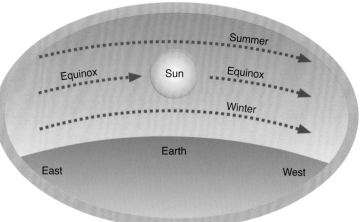

▲ The Earth spins from east to west, so the Sun rises in the east and sets in the west. The three blue dotted lines show the position of the Sun above the horizon in a temperate location such as the United Kingdom.

snake shape shadow

snake's head carving

▼ At sunrise and sunset on the **equinox** at this temple in Mexico, the sunlight forms the shape of a snake on the side of the staircase. This shape is not seen at any other time of year.

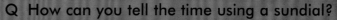

Q and A

Equinox

The word equinox means equal day and night. In the temperate zone there are two equinoxes each year, which occur when the Sun is over the Equator. The vernal or spring equinox occurs in March and the autumnal equinox occurs in September.

Q How can you tell the time using a sundial?

A A sundial consists of a stick that casts a shadow on to a flat surface marked with lines that show the time of day. The position of the shadow is used to tell the time.

▲ This sundial shows the time to be about 3 o'clock.

▲ The spring equinox is when the popular festival of Hanami takes place in Japan. Hanami, or 'flower viewing', celebrates the end of winter and when the first flowers appear on the cherry trees.

Solstice

In the Northern Hemisphere, the longest day of the year is 21 June. This is called the **summer solstice** and it occurs when the Sun is at its furthest point north from the Equator. Traditionally, it marks the first day of summer. The **winter solstice** is the shortest day, when the Sun is lowest in the sky and this occurs on 21 December.

Spring

Spring is a time of change. The Sun rises higher above the horizon and the days grow longer. There is more heat in the Sun because it lies overhead, so the days become warmer.

Becoming active

Many animals spend the winter months in caves and other sheltered places to escape the cold winter weather. In spring, they emerge and become active again. Spring is also the time when lots of plants start to grow, the first flowers appear and the first butterflies of spring fly on the warm, sunny days.

▲ The flowers of fruit trees, like this apple blossom, open in spring.

▶ Spring is the start of the farming year, when farmers plough their fields to break up the soil so that crops can be sown.

Q and A

Q What is the dawn chorus?

A It is early morning birdsong. Birds sing more in spring as it is the start of their breeding season. The time that many sing is at daybreak, or dawn, and the chorus reaches a peak in early May, when male birds sing to attract females and to warn other males to stay away.

New life

When the days become longer, many animals change their behaviour. For many animals, the warmer days with more hours of daylight are the trigger to start to **breed**. Breeding in spring is important, because it means that many young animals are born at the start of summer when there is plenty of food. For example, in spring, frogs and toads return to their breeding ponds to lay their eggs. Their tadpoles feed on small plants and animals in the water.

▼ Sheep give birth to lambs in spring. This ewe has twin lambs.

▲ A male robin sings to attract a mate.

Summer

In temperate climates, summer is a period of long, warm days. The Sun reaches its highest point in the sky where its heat warms the air, and there is less rain.

Making food

In summer, there is plenty of sunlight for plants to make their food. Plants have a **pigment** in their leaves called **chlorophyll**. The chlorophyll traps **light energy** which is used to combine **carbon dioxide** from the air and water from the soil to form sugars and oxygen. This process is called **photosynthesis**. The plant uses the sugars to fuel growth.

▼ Towards the end of summer cereal plants produce seeds, using the food that they make in their leaves.

▼ Plants use sugar to make **nectar** in their flowers. This attracts insects, such as butterflies, which **pollinate** the flower.

Q and A

Lots of food

With plenty of food in summer, young animals grow quickly. **Larvae** of insects, such as caterpillars, feed on young leaves. These insects are often hunted by parent birds who feed them to their fast-growing chicks. Young birds are food for other **predators** such as birds of prey, foxes and badgers. This forms a **food chain**.

Q Why do **anticyclones** bring good weather in summer?

A An anticyclone occurs when there is a large area of air that is sinking towards the ground. This creates **high pressure**, which brings gentle winds and clear, sunny weather. The anticyclone moves very slowly and pushes away clouds that bring rain.

▶ The female fox, or vixen, hunts small animals to feed her cubs.

Summer storms

The high temperatures may cause summer thunderstorms. The sunshine warms the ground and currents of warm air rise into the atmosphere. The air cools and **water vapour condenses** to form droplets that build up into huge banks of clouds. Strong currents of air swirl around inside the clouds, smashing water droplets together and building up **static electricity** that causes lightning.

▲ Storm clouds form on very hot days and bring heavy rain.

17

Autumn

Autumn is a time of shortening days, and mornings are often frosty. The Sun is lower in the sky and sunset occurs earlier each day. The air temperature drops and there is more rainfall. The shorter days are a signal to many plants and animals to prepare for winter.

Leaf fall

Deciduous trees drop their leaves in autumn to survive the winter. This is because there is less sunlight to make food and the colder temperatures mean that trees cannot get enough water from the frozen ground. Also, their branches weigh less without leaves and are less likely to be broken by snowfall. The trees regrow their leaves in spring.

▶ Toadstools, such as these fly agaric, appear in autumn after warm, wet weather. Toadstools are **fungi** and they feed on the fallen leaves on the ground.

Q Why do leaves change colour in autumn?
A Before a deciduous tree drops its leaves, it removes all the valuable substances that it can use again. For example, it takes the chlorophyll that gives the leaves their green appearance. When the pigment is broken down, the green colour is lost and other pigments can be seen, such as **carotene**, which has an orange-red colour.

▲ Many farmers are busy in the autumn bringing in the harvest.

Collecting food

Animals prepare for winter, too. Some, such as squirrels, gather nuts and fruits that are plentiful in autumn and store them in the ground for the coming months. Other animals eat lots of food to build up layers of fat under their skin, so they too can survive the long, cold months.

▶ Red squirrels collect nuts and store them in piles on the ground to eat during the winter.

▲ Autumn leaves.

Winter

Winter is the season of short days, long nights and colder weather. The Sun is low over the horizon and so not much heat reaches the ground.

▲ Frost is a covering of ice that forms on exposed surfaces when the air temperature falls below freezing.

Frost and ice

Frost forms on clear nights, when the lack of cloud cover means heat is lost from the ground into the atmosphere and temperatures fall below freezing. As the air is chilled, water vapour in the air condenses on to surfaces where it freezes. During extremely cold weather, temperatures may fall well below freezing. Ice forms on lakes, ponds and even on rivers, while oil freezes in car engines. At very low temperatures, even steel becomes brittle and breaks.

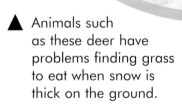

▲ Animals such as these deer have problems finding grass to eat when snow is thick on the ground.

Snowfall

In winter there are heavy snowfalls over mountains and in the temperate regions, especially northern areas such as Canada and Siberia. Snowflakes, which form in clouds, are made from many ice crystals stuck together.

◀ Snowflakes usually melt before they reach the ground. But if it is cold enough, the snowflakes fall as snow and settle.

Q What is a blizzard?

A A blizzard is a snow storm with strong winds and low temperatures. The heavy snowfall swirling around in the wind makes it difficult to see very far.

▼ Skiers like powdery snow as it is easier for them to make turns and control their speed.

▲ A bison standing in a blizzard.

Types of snow

There are different types of snow. Powdery snow, the type favoured by skiers, is dry snow made from small ice crystals. This forms in very cold conditions. Wet snow forms when temperatures are closer to freezing point. The snowflakes are large and melt quickly.

Dry and wet seasons

Temperate zones have four seasons, but parts of the tropics have only two seasons: a dry season and a wet season.

Tropical grasslands

The vast tropical grasslands, or **savannahs**, of Southern Africa are warm all year round. During the wet season, the Sun heats the ground, causing warm air to rise and form clouds. Large thunderclouds bring heavy downpours. This rain is important as it enables the grass to grow, providing food for grazing animals. Then the rains stop and the dry season begins. This season is cooler with clear, sunny days. Water becomes scarce as water holes disappear and rivers run dry.

▼ Thunderclouds gather over the African savannah.

▶ A giraffe drinks from a pool of water during the dry season.

Q and A

Migration

Huge herds of grazing animals, such as wildebeest and zebras, live on the savannah. Each year they travel long distances or **migrate** in search of fresh grass. When grass and water disappear in one area, the herds travel to areas where there is rain and fresh grazing.

Q How do elephants know where to go for fresh water?

A The rumble of thunder creates vibrations in the ground that the elephants detect with their sensitive toes. They know thunderstorms bring rain so they walk towards the thunder to find water.

▼ Migrating wildebeest take the same circular route each year, covering a distance of almost 3,000 kilometres.

▲ Elephants can feel the rumble of thunder across long distances.

Monsoons

A **monsoon climate** is found in South and South-East Asia and parts of northern Australia. It has three seasons: cool and dry, hot and dry, and wet with **torrential rain**.

Monsoon winds

In a monsoon climate, the seasons change when the wind changes direction. In much of India, the winter is hot and dry because a dry wind blows from the north-west. In summer, the winds change direction and come from the south-west, picking up water from the surface of the Indian Ocean. When they reach land, the water vapour condenses and huge clouds build up. There is torrential rain from June to September, followed by a couple of months of cool, dry weather.

▲ During the monsoon rains in South-East Asia, daily life goes on as normal.

24

Q and A

Rainfall

The monsoon rains are vitally important to India, despite the damage from flooding and landslides that the heavy rains often cause. These rains bring 80 per cent of India's annual rainfall. The water fills the rivers that are used for drinking water, watering crops and generating electricity. Without the rain, rivers would run dry and crops, such as rice, would fail.

Q Why was the 2008 monsoon in India unusual?

A The monsoon rains usually reach Delhi, the capital of India, on or about the 29 June each year. In 2008, the rains started on 15 June, two weeks earlier than usual. This broke a 108-year-old record.

▼ During the dry season, farmers plough the soil and get ready to plant their crops once the rain returns.

▲ Monsoon rains in India.

25

Surviving extremes

Plants and animals have many ways of surviving extreme weather such as cold winters and hot, dry summers.

Desert survival

Deserts lack water, so plants and animals have to find ways of finding and storing water so they can survive until the next rains. When desert pools dry up, the desert spadefoot toad digs a burrow deep in the sand and only comes out when it rains again. Lizards shelter in burrows or under the sand when it is hot and emerge at night to feed.

▼ Cacti, like this barrel cactus, grow in deserts. They have stems that can expand to store water.

▼ This plant growing in the Sahara Desert of North Africa has long roots to take up water and to anchor it in the sand.

Q and A

Flying away

In winter, many birds migrate to warmer places to escape the cold weather. Bewick swans, for example, fly from Russia to England for the winter, while swallows fly from Europe to Africa.

Q Which animal has the longest migration?

A The Arctic tern. This tiny bird leaves the Arctic in autumn and flies south to the Antarctic where it spends the summer months. Then it flies back to the Arctic, a total journey of about 35,000 km.

Surviving cold

Small **mammals**, such as hedgehogs and dormice, need to eat a lot of food every day to stay warm. Food is often in short supply in winter, so they **hibernate** in a warm, dry place. The animals emerge again in spring when the temperature rises. Mammals, such as bears and squirrels, do not hibernate all winter, but come out on warmer days to feed.

▲ Arctic tern.

▼ Small mammals, like this edible dormouse, eat lots of nuts in autumn. They hibernate during winter and survive on the fat stored in their body.

Climate change

Around the world, **climate change** means that weather patterns are more difficult to predict. This is caused by global warming.

Global warming

Global warming is the gradual increase in the temperature at the Earth's surface and it is caused by an increase in greenhouse gases. These are gases, such as carbon dioxide and **methane**, which trap heat in the Earth's atmosphere. It is their increase that causes the temperature to rise.

▲ The survival of polar bears is threatened because Arctic summers are becoming warmer. This is causing the ice to melt.

Global changes

Climate change is affecting the weather around the world. Some places are becoming warmer than usual and rainfall is less predictable. For example, in southern Spain the spring is arriving earlier each year. Extreme weather is becoming more common, too. There are more storms and torrential rain in the Caribbean, and more droughts in places such as East Africa and Australia.

▶ This power station burns coal which releases lots of carbon dioxide into the atmosphere.

Q and A

Surviving change

Plants and animals have to cope with the effects that these changes have on their environment. Some animals are benefitting from warmer climates. For example, some butterflies have been found further north than usual because the mild winters enable them to survive. Sadly, other animals, such as the caribou and Arctic fox, are disappearing, as they cannot find enough food.

Q How do **corals** tell us about past climates?

A Scientists have found ways of dating corals and analysing their hard skeletons. They have examined corals that are hundreds of years old and worked out the ocean temperature and sea levels of the past. This helps scientists to show that global warming is really happening now.

▶ The comma butterfly is extending its range north as winters become milder.

▶ Badgers suffer during very dry summers as they cannot find enough worms in the ground.

▲ Stone coral.

Glossary

anticlockwise moving in a direction that is opposite to the movement of the hands of a clock

anticyclone the atmospheric conditions that occur when the air is sinking over an area

atmosphere the protective layer of gases around the Earth

breed to reproduce; to produce young

carbon dioxide a gas found in the air. Carbon dioxide is a greenhouse gas, which means it contributes to global warming

carotene an orange-red coloured substance found in plants

chlorophyll the green substance in plant leaves, used in photosynthesis

climate the regular pattern of weather that occurs in a particular place over a long period of time

climate change a change in the regular pattern of weather that occurs in an area

condense to change from gas to liquid

coral a small marine animal that has a stony skeleton

current a flow of water or air in a particular direction

deciduous trees trees that drop their leaves in autumn

Equator the imaginary line around the centre of the Earth, between the North and South poles

equinox the time of year when the days and nights are of equal length - ie 12 hours long. The vernal (spring) equinox occurs in March, and the autumnal equinox in September

food chain the feeding relationships between a sequence of organisms

fungi organisms that are neither animal nor plant. Many fungi help to break down dead matter in the ground

hibernate to go into a state of complete rest or become totally inactive in order to survive a cold winter

high pressure when a mass of air is sinking and pushing down on the surface of the Earth, producing hot sunny days in summer or cold frosty days in winter

larva (plural larvae) the growing stage of an animal such as an insect

light energy energy from the Sun

mammal an animal that has a backbone and is covered with hair. The females give birth to live young and feed them with milk

methane a colourless gas found in the atmosphere. It is a greenhouse gas like carbon dioxide

migrate to make a regular journey that is often linked with changes in the seasons

monsoon climate a climate which experiences a season of torrential rain

nectar a sugary liquid found in flowers

Northern Hemisphere the part of the world to the north of the Equator

orbit the path of one object around another in space, for example a planet moving round the Sun

photosynthesis the process by which plants make their food

pigment a coloured substance such as chlorophyll

poles the most northerly and southerly parts of the Earth

pollinate to carry pollen from one flower to another

predator an animal that hunts other animals for food

reflect when light bounces off a surface

savannah another name for tropical grassland

season a part of the year, such as spring, summer, autumn and winter

Southern Hemisphere the part of the world to the south of the Equator

static electricity the build up of electrical charges on an object. For example, a crackle of static electricity may be produced when you run a plastic comb through your hair

summer solstice the longest day of the year

temperate zone part of the world that lies between the tropics and the poles where there are seasons and the climate is mild for much of the year

torrential rain very heavy rain

tropics the regions of the Earth that lie close to the Equator. They experience hot and often humid weather when the air is very damp

Vikings seafaring people from Scandinavia who lived from the eighth to eleventh centuries

water vapour water in the form of a gas

winter solstice the shortest day of the year

Further reading

Earthwise: Seasons, Jim Pipe (Franklin Watts 2008)
Global Warming, Science at the Edge, Sally Morgan (Heinemann Library 2009)
This is My Planet: A Guide to Global Warming, Jan Thornhill (Franklin Watts, 2011)

Websites

Weather Wiz Kids: www.weatherwizkids.com
Climate change: www.epa.gov/climatechange/kids/index.html
Endangered animals: www.kidsplanet.org

Index